GOD'S TRIANGLE OF FINANCIAL PROSPERITY

3 KEYS TO PROSPER NOW, COME OUT OF DEBT AND HAVE MORE THAN ENOUGH

FRANCIS JONAH

IMPORTANT

My name is Francis Jonah. I believe all things are possible. It is because of this belief that I have achieved so much in life. This belief extends to all. I believe every human being is equipped to succeed in every circumstance, regardless of the circumstance.

I know the only gap that exists between you and what you need to achieve or overcome is knowledge.

People are destroyed for lack of knowledge.

It is for this reason that I write short practical books that are so simple, people begin to experience immediate results as evidenced by the many testimonies I receive on a daily basis for my various books.

This book is no exception. You will obtain results because of it.

Visit my website for powerful articles and materials

www.francisjonah.com

FREE GIFTS

Just to say Thank You for downloading my book, I'd like to give you these books for free.

Download these 4 powerful books today for free and give yourself a great future.

Click Here to Download

Your testimonies will abound. Click Here to see my other books. They have produced many testimonies and I want your testimony to be one too.

Counselling Or Prayer

Send me an email if you need prayer or counsel or you have a question.

Better still if you want to make my acquaintance

My email is drfrancisjonah@gmail.com

Other books by Francis Jonah

1. 3 Day Fasting Challenge: How to receive manifestation of answers

2. How to Have Outrageous Financial Abundance In No Time:Biblical Principles For Immediate And Overwhelming Financial Success

3. 5 Bible Promises, Prayers and Decrees That Will Give You The Best Year Ever: A book for Shaping Every Year Successfully plus devotional (Book Of Promises 1)

4. Influencing The Unseen Realm: How to Influence The Spirit Realm for Victory in The Physical Realm(Spiritual Success Books)

5. [Prayer That Works: Taking Responsibility For Answered Prayer](#)

6. [Healing The Sick In Five Minutes:How Anyone Can Heal Any Sickness](#)

7. [The Financial Miracle Prayer](#)

8. [The Best Secret To Answered Prayer](#)

9. [The Believer's Authority(Authority Of The Believer,Power And Authority Of The Believer)](#)

10. [The Healing Miracle Prayer](#)

11. I Shall Not Die: Secrets To Long Life And Overcoming The Fear of Death

12. Three Straightforward Steps To Outrageous Financial Abundance: Personal Finance (Finance Made Easy Book 1)

13. Prayers For Financial Miracles: And 3 Ways To Receive Answers Quickly

14. Book: 3 Point Blueprint For Building Strong Faith: Spiritual:Religious:Christian:Motivational

15. How To Stop Sinning Effortlessly

16. The Power Of Faith-Filled Words

17. All Sin Is Paid For: An Eye Opening Book

18. Be Happy Now:No More Depression

19. The Ultimate Christian: How To Win In Every Life Situation: A book full of Revelations

20. Books:How To Be Free From Sicknesses And Diseases(Divine Health): Divine Health Scriptures

21. Multiply Your Personal Income In Less Than 30 Days

22. Ultimate Method To Memorize The Bible Quickly: (How To Learn Scripture Memorization)

23. Overcoming Emotional Abuse

24. Passing Exams The Easy Way: 90% and above in exams (Learning Simplified)

25. Books:Goal Setting For Those In A Hurry To Achieve Fast

26. Do Something Lest You Do Nothing

27. Financial Freedom:My Personal Blue-Print Made Easy For Men And Women

28. Why Men Go To Hell

29. Budgeting Tools And How My Budget Makes Me More Money

30. How To Raise Capital In 72 Hours: Quickly and Effectively Raise Capital Easily in Unconventional Ways (Finance Made Easy)

31. How To Love Unconditionally

32. Financial Independence: The Simple Path I Used To Wealth

33. Finding Happiness: The Story Of John Miller: A Christian Fiction

34. Finance Made Easy (2 Book Series)

Click here to see my author page

CONTENT

INTRODUCTION

CHAPTER ONE..................................

CHAPTER TWO..................................

CHAPTER THREE................................

CHAPTER FOUR..................................

CHAPTER FIVE..................................

INTRODUCTION

Poverty is not a mystery. It is very easy to know why people are poor. Every wise man understands that knowing the cause of a problem is half the problem solved.

Many poor people do not know why they are poor and thus it is difficult for them to enjoy financial prosperity. Poverty is thus a mystery to them.

Knowing why people are poor thus is half the problem of financial prosperity solved. This is because you will know not to fall in that trap.

The Bible makes it clear that the reason people are poor is because they refuse instruction.

Pro 13:18 Poverty and shame shall be to him that refuseth instruction: but he that regardeth reproof shall be honoured.

Proverbs 13:18

Every poor person is poor because of a refusal of instructions. Which instructions have you refused?

Those instructions you have refused are the very reasons for your poverty or lack of financial prosperity.

The Bible is clear on it. Two things, shame and poverty shall come to those who refuse instruction. God loves you and has opened your eyes to a fundamental problem of all human beings. This is a serious revelation.

This book will give you three foundational instructions, which we will refer to as keys that will cause you to begin your journey of financial prosperity.

It will settle any doubt in your mind as to whether you are on the right path or not to financial prosperity. It will give you the confidence to run with the discoveries you will make and cause you to enter into a realm of absolute financial prosperity.

You will so prosper that, it will take only yourself to sabotage the prosperity that will come to you. You can never be poor again if you practise the keys that will be given to you in this book.

Let us delve into the revelations herein and come out better financially. We will start with the power of the triangle as it relates to your financial prosperity. It is a fundamental concept you must understand before you get into the meat of the keys to help you prosper financially.

CHAPTER ONE

THE POWER OF THE TRIANGLE

Let us understand this basic concept so that we can use it to establish our keys to financial prosperity.

A triangle has three sides. God's triangle of prosperity also has three sides.

Each of the three sides of God's triangle of financial prosperity represents something that must be done so that the triangle will operate efficiently to your advantage.

Once you establish your own triangle, using the three parameters that will be explained to you, your prosperity will begin to be visible automatically.

One parameter on its own can get you to a certain level of financial prosperity, but all three working together will ensure tremendous financial success.

They ensure a multiplier effect far greater than can ever be imagined.

This is what the impact of the triangle looks like:

10x10 is just 100 but add a third parameter and you enter into another dimension of results

10x10x10 = 1000

The figure (10) multiplied 3 times (triangle) takes a person immediately to the realm of the thousands.

Imagine what it can do to the figure 100.

You will also enjoy the tremendous success the triangle brings in Jesus' name.

The mystery of the number "3"

Another reason the triangle of financial prosperity does tremendous things for anyone who establishes it in their lives is because of the mystery of the number three.

Three is the number of wholeness. It is the number of God.

Most of the powerful things on earth are in three's. There are many examples that back this up.

God is Father, Son and Spirit. He accomplishes the fullness of His purpose in the trinity.

1Jn 5:7 For there are three that bear record in heaven, the Father, the Word, and the Holy Ghost: and these three are one.

1 John 5:7

This scripture shows the three, which bear record in heaven. Do you see the number three?

We measure time on three planes. The past, which refers to things that have happened, the present, which refers to things that are happening and the future, which refers to things which will happen. With these three planes, time receives its wholeness of operation.

Heb 13:8 Jesus Christ the same yesterday, and to day, and for ever.

Hebrews 13:8

The scripture clearly shows the three dimensions of time.

The world we live in consists of three forms. The air, the land and the waters. With these three forms, creation on earth is fully accommodated.

Gen 1:28 And God blessed them, and God said unto them, Be fruitful, and multiply, and replenish the earth, and subdue it: and have dominion over the fish of the sea, and over the fowl of the air, and over every living thing that moveth upon the earth.

Genesis 1:28

Based on the scripture above, you can easily see the three forms that accommodate the world we live in.

There are three parts of a man. The body, the soul and the spirit. With these three parts, man is fully equipped to function.

1Th 5:23 And the very God of peace sanctify you wholly; and I pray God your whole spirit and soul and body be preserved blameless unto the coming of our Lord Jesus Christ.

1 Thessalonians 5:23

The scripture above shows the three parts that make every human being. Still reinforcing the power of three.

There are three things which abide according to the Bible, faith hope and love and love is the greatest of them all.

1Co 13:13 And now abideth faith, hope, charity, these three; but the greatest of these is charity

1 Corinthians 13:13

These few examples go to show the mystery behind the number three and why the triangle of God's financial prosperity will guarantee your own financial prosperity.

Let us discover another important thing about the triangle so we can zoom into building our own triangle.

The triangle is the most stable shape

The triangle is said to be the most stable shape on earth. It is so strong and stable that it can hardly be displaced. It thus serves as a strong platform or foundation for things to be built.

Your principles of growth can be built on the triangle.

Your principles of business can be built on the platform of the triangle.

Your principles of marriage success can be built on the triangle.

This is the reason I know the triangle of God's financial prosperity is on solid ground and will guarantee great success in your financial life.

Now that we know the power of the triangle, let us establish the three sides of God's triangle for financial prosperity so that we can build our own triangle.

It is important that you understand each parameter of the triangle and not just knowing what it is. It is the understanding of these parameters that will bring you maximum results.

For this reason, read and understand each side of the triangle carefully in the coming chapters. Let's move on to the next chapter.

CHAPTER TWO

THE PLACE OF WORK

Work is the first side of God's triangle of prosperity. It is the base of that triangle and the foundation of your financial prosperity.

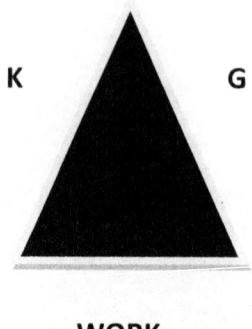

WORK

It is the first parameter you must establish for yourself in implementing your triangle of prosperity. We will talk more about the subject of work in this chapter but before then, we will digress a little into why we work because many people are ignorant of this subject.

There are many who do not know why they work. This lack of knowledge is the reason for most of the financial problems they face.

The wrong understanding of why we work has led many people to poverty and financial struggles.

It is only the right understanding that will make sure these problems are settled.

Why do we work?

God is so good that He tells us the reason why we work in the book of Ephesians:

Eph 4:28 Let him that stole steal no more: but rather let him labour, working with his hands the thing which is good, that he may have to give to him that needeth.

Ephesians 4:28

We are told clearly here that we work so that we can have to give. If you lacked that knowledge, thank God you have it today.

It simply means, we work to give. The reason we work to give is simple: our financial prosperity is not in the work, it is in the giving. It starts from the work, which is the foundation. However, the giving is the catalyst.

We work to give

It is our giving that causes our finances to be multiplied.

This is the reason many people work for so many years yet have nothing.

It is simply because they think they are working to take care of themselves.

They will therefore spend everything they earn on themselves and give little or nothing out claiming that what they have is not enough.

Even when what you earn is not enough, you should know why you work and make giving a priority.

You are working to have in order to give so that you can prosper financially.

This is what has entrapped many people in poverty. Their budgets have no place for giving, only their personal expenses.

Don't keep making that mistake, make room for giving regularly.

God is wiser than man

The Bible says that the foolishness of God is wiser than the wisdom of man. How much more the wisdom of God?

If God in His wisdom tells us in His word that we work to give, we must walk by this wisdom and we will be sure to prosper financially.

1Co 1:25 Because the foolishness of God is wiser than men; and the weakness of God is stronger than men.

1 Corinthians 1:25

It is only those who think they are wiser than God that go contrary to such a charge and suffer painfully for it.

I know you will not be counted amongst that lot.

Are you working to give or you are working to eat?

With that said, are you the kind that works to eat or you are the kind that works to give?

Quickly identify where you are and reposition yourself if need be.

It is important to renew your mind in this particular thing because it is the foundation for greater financial success.

Let us get back to the foundation of God's triangle of financial prosperity, which is work.

Your work is the avenue you create to receive financial inflows

The work you do is the avenue you create for finances to flow into your life. Thus the more avenues you create, the more money flows your way.

Even God blesses the work of our hand:

Deu 28:12 The LORD shall open unto thee his good treasure, the heaven to give the rain unto thy land in his season, and to bless all the work of thine hand: and thou shalt lend unto many nations, and thou shalt not borrow

Deuteronomy 28:12.

If we understand the role of work in our financial prosperity, we will put in extra effort in the area of work.

If a man works from 8am to 12 pm and takes $500 weekly.

And another works from 8am to 12 pm at the same place and takes $500, then goes to work at another place from 2pm to 8pm and takes another $500, it is easy to note the person who has created more avenues for financial inflow.

It is also easy to know the one who will have more money at the end of the week.

Work is the foundation for financial prosperity.

This is why the Bible says the one that does not work must not eat.

2Th 3:10 For even when we were with you, this we commanded you, that if any would not work, neither should he eat.

2 Thessalonians 3:10

It was a direct command that those who did not work should not eat. Beloved, work is very important.

It is the foundation of your financial prosperity. Do not take it for granted. Are you working hard enough?

Hardwork

Now that you know why you work and the truth that the foundation of your financial success is work, you must now encounter the place of hard work.

Hard work cannot be overemphasized. It is a master key to financial prosperity.

The Bible clearly makes us understand that lazy people will not prosper financially. The hardworking will prosper in their finances.

Pro 10:4 He becometh poor that dealeth with a slack hand: but the hand of the diligent maketh rich.

Proverbs 10:4

God is so good and faithful. He has given us truths that will liberate us from poverty.

The lazy person will be poor.

The hardworking person will be rich. It is a statement of truth and must be accepted and worked on for profitable results.

Under normal circumstances, a farmer who works on 10 acres will make more money than the farmer who works on one acre.

The difference between a man that farms one acre and another man that farms 10 acres is hard work.

When you put in maximum effort and time, you will certainly come back with results.

A successful man once told me, whatever you put time and effort in will work.

Work hard and you will prosper financially.

The dilemma of poverty and hard work

There is a little dilemma that I need to point out so that many can escape that trap.

Rich people normally work more than poor people do. Rich people most of the time before they became rich worked more than 12 hours a day. Sometimes way after they have become rich, they continue to work more than 12 hours a day

Many people work about 8 hours in a day. And even when working, they do not put in their maximum.

I used to work 16 hours daily until I hit the financial target I wanted. If you are poor and do not work that long, then that is your problem found for you.

One of the most common reasons poor people work less is that, they do not get the kind of results (money) equal to the work they put in, so they put in less work. Others are just lazy and thus do not improve their financial fortunes.

Somehow, because the rich make more from the work they do, they continue to work harder to make more money.

It is time you understand that hard work is important for financial prosperity. Are you working as hard as you are capable of? God and those who depend on you require that of you.

Ideas for more work

I remember one of the best pieces of advice I read somewhere.

It said, instead of finding a second job. Build a part-time business.

One of the best ways to work harder is to find or create a part time business and put in the necessary work to make it successful.

There are many profitable part time businesses. Find the right one and make it work. How do you find one? Talk to people who are already into successful business, go on google and YouTube which are excellent search engines to get as much information as you can.

A word of caution, do not explore these three options and come back saying you didn't find an opportunity, it will mean you were lazy in the simplest of steps in getting a profitable extra stream of income.

I have seen many people exhibit such laziness and it is not funny at all.

Understand that even finding the right part time business is work. It is work that many do shabbily or quit at the first attempt.

Brethren, hard work is the foundation of financial prosperity. Get it right. Go all out and come back with results that will make God and your family proud of you. Talk less of your generation.

Why all billionaires have businesses

All billionaires have businesses because of the truth that work is the foundation of financial prosperity.

A business employs many people and thus ensures that many are working for the owner of the business.

The work of all these employees is what ensures the financial success of the billionaire.

Some businesspersons have thousands of people working for them. No wonder they make so much money.

If the foundation of financial prosperity is work. Then, all things being equal, the man who has 50 people working for him stands a greater chance of prospering financially than a man who is working alone for his financial success.

This is the reason every billionaire owns a business. The business helps them employ people who work for them.

The work of all these people causes them to prosper financially. That is enough motivation to start and succeed in a business too.

What if you are already working hard?

If you are working hard and still not gotten to the level of financial prosperity you want, then remember that there are two other sides of the triangle that must be implemented.

Before that, you must have explored the option of more work or a part-time business.

Let us move into the second triangle and see how it can help you.

CHAPTER THREE

THE PLACE OF KNOWLEDGE

Knowledge is the second side of God's triangle of prosperity. It is the parameter that must be added after you have established your foundation of work.

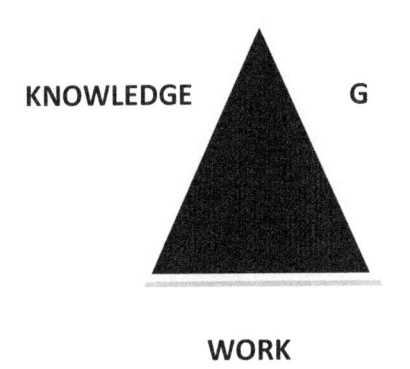

KNOWLEDGE　　　G

WORK

I am confident that, at this stage, you have already written down what you will do about the work parameter in your financial prosperity triangle.

There are any people working very hard, but working without knowledge. This means they are only employing one side of the prosperity triangle.

They have not yet established the knowledge parameter of their triangle.

To prosper financially, there is the need for knowledge. The bible clearly states that people of God perish because they lack knowledge.

Hos 4:6 My people are destroyed for lack of knowledge: because thou hast rejected knowledge, I will also reject thee, that thou shalt

be no priest to me: seeing thou hast forgotten the law of thy God, I will also forget thy children.

Hosea 4:6

Many people are stuck at their level of income because they are not investing in knowledge. They are operating at the same level of results because they have not invested in relevant knowledge.

Relevant knowledge that will make them earn more from the time and effort they are putting into their work.

Their businesses are stagnant because they have not increased their knowledge. They do not know how to attract more customers, they do not know how to retain the customers, they do not know how to make their customers buy more products.

They are operating with the knowledge they had 10 years ago, which was passed on to them from a TV commercial.

Ignorance has thus become a killer of their financial destinies. The lack of desire to pursue the knowledge that will transform their finances has become a stumbling block to their financial prosperity.

Acquire knowledge or fail

When two people are doing the same thing, the one with the superior knowledge will always excel.

Two companies can be selling the same product yet one of the companies can do better than the other because of their level of knowledge.

The place of knowledge should never be underestimated in the financial prosperity equation.

It is essential beyond what anyone can think. Make the acquisition of knowledge a priority and it will be the game changer you have always wanted.

Knowledge is better than choice gold

Many people are crying for money. They need more money.

Such people do not know that they do not even know the root of their problem.

Anyone that needs money has a bigger problem than money. Their problem is a lack of relevant knowledge and not the lack of money.

The Bible clearly makes us understand this truth:

Pro 8:10 Receive my instruction, and not silver; and knowledge rather than choice gold.

Proverbs 8:10

God says choose knowledge over the best of gold or money. The reason is simple. The one who has relevant knowledge can always get the choicest of gold at any time they want.

If you have choice gold without knowledge, you will spend the choice gold and have nothing left.

This is the reason God asks us to choose knowledge over choice gold.

Any man who has knowledge about how to multiply money will not chase money. Money will chase them. Even with one dollar, they can multiply it into thousands of dollars.

The one who lacks knowledge about how to multiply money will spend and finish 1 million dollars that is put in their account free of charge.

The money that will make you prosper financially has passed through your hands several times. Instead of multiplying it, you spent or saved it. You spent or saved it because you lacked knowledge to multiply that $100 or that $1000.

It is time to be wise. Establish the knowledge dimension of your prosperity triangle. Learn the laws of money. Know how to multiply money and with this knowledge you will soar higher and higher financially.

Struggling until knowledge came

I started a business and failed miserably in it until I decided to acquire knowledge.

After watching over 40 videos and reading over 30 books on the business I was doing, I began to see my results increase. My finances increased as a result.

I was doing the work and getting little results. I was working very hard but with little knowledge.

When I added knowledge to the work I was doing, things turned out to be so much better. I became financially comfortable.

There are too many people stuck at the work dimension with little results to show financially. It is time to add the knowledge parameter.

When was the last time you acquired knowledge to improve what you are doing?

When was the last time you acquired knowledge to help you prosper financially?

When was the last time you acquired knowledge on how to increase your customers, revenue or profits?

When was the last time you acquired knowledge on how God prospers people financially.

The knowledge parameter is very critical and has been a major separator between those who succeed and those who fail.

Become a pursuer of knowledge and things will turn out well for you and your financial prosperity will show for all to see and appreciate.

I pray that for you in Jesus' name. Receive the strength and desire to pursue the knowledge that will transform your finances. God lead you to the right knowledge in Jesus' name.

The story of the boys in business

I know five young men who all started a business.

They all worked very hard in their businesses. There was something peculiar about one of the boys though, he always went for paid seminars and studied all he could study. The rest of the boys just spent their spare time watching movies.

Weekend seminars soon became his daily habit. He became a knowledge addict.

Two years later, his business empire was bigger than all the four other young men combined.

What had made the difference? It was knowledge. Beloved knowledge will expand your financial fortunes.

The knowledge parameter he added to his work had separated him from his colleagues by far.

To know how the parameter of knowledge is critical for financial prosperity, look at this scripture:

Pro 24:4 And by knowledge shall the chambers be filled with all precious and pleasant riches.

Proverbs 24:4

For your chambers to be filled with all precious and pleasant riches, go for knowledge. It is a powerful key.

Your riches will be pleasant and precious if you pursue knowledge. Can you incorporate 30 minutes every day to pursue knowledge on how you can prosper financially?

There is knowledge out there that will transform your life. Seek it and you shall find.

Mat 7:7 Ask, and it shall be given you; seek, and ye shall find; knock, and it shall be opened unto you:

Mat 7:8 For every one that asketh receiveth; and he that seeketh findeth; and to him that knocketh it shall be opened.

Matthew 7:7-8

Everyone who seeks finds. When you seek knowledge, you will find it and it will give you pleasant riches.

Glory to God. I see you establishing the second parameter of your financial prosperity aggressively.

Your problem is knowledge and not money. Pursue knowledge.

Knowledge will multiply your money and business

One of the most painful experiences of my life was when I lived for years without knowing how to multiply the money I earned from my work.

I just spent the money and waited for the next salary to come. It was all because I lacked the knowledge of how to multiply the money that came my way. Do not go through that too. Get knowledge.

Don't let your business struggle unnecessarily because you lack knowledge. Get relevant knowledge and you will see your financial situation change as you apply the knowledge.

Keep pursuing and applying knowledge till you find the right knowledge that will help you. Too many people quit after applying a piece of knowledge and it doesn't give them the results they need.

Beloved, it is knowledge that will bring your prosperity. If one piece of knowledge doesn't work, find another and apply.

At all cost, you must established the parameter of knowledge because it is profitable to you

When you have established these two parameters, there is a third and final parameter you must put in place.

This parameter is what will ensure that you never become poor again in your life. Let us move into the next chapter to learn all about this last parameter.

Many people have slacked in this area and it has affected them badly. To the glory of God, you will correct this parameter in your life so that you can confidently grow and manifest financial prosperity at its highest level.

My desire is to see your progress, prosperity and freedom from negative people and circumstances. Because of that, please permit me to introduce two courses that I believe passionately will help you.

1. To cure prayerlessness, an inconsistent prayer life and the pain of not enjoying all that God has made available to you,, click here to learn more about my 3 Day Course on "How to Overcome prayerlessness" that will solve the problem of prayerlessness in your life.

2.To overcome the pain of not having enough money to live where you want, eat what you want to eat and be a blessing to the multitudes around you, I have created a _7 Day Financial Abundance Course_ that will deliver financial abundance to you quickly.

Click _here_ to learn more about that course.

You will see increase and enlargement as you step out in faith.

CHAPTER FOUR

THE PLACE OF GIVING

Giving is the third side of God's triangle of prosperity. It must be added after the parameters of work and knowledge have been established. This parameter completes God's triangle of financial prosperity.

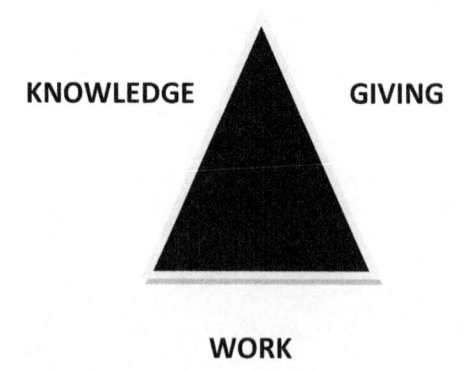

```
        KNOWLEDGE   ▲   GIVING
                   ▲▲▲
                  ▲▲▲▲▲
                 ▲▲▲▲▲▲▲
                   WORK
```

Many people ignore this part of the financial prosperity formula and suffer badly for it.

The truth is that giving is what multiplies people's finances beyond their wildest imagination. It engages the divine laws on behalf of the giver.

The Bible clearly states that:

Luk 6:38 Give, and it shall be given unto you; good measure, pressed down, and shaken together, and running over, shall men give into your bosom. For with the same measure that ye mete withal it shall be measured to you again.

Luke 6:38

This clearly shows that when you give, what you gave is multiplied back to you. The process is like this a good measure of what you have given is taken, pressed down, running over and given back to you.

This is a marvellous law. It produces tremendous results and if you know God, you know that His laws do not fail.

When you understand this law, you will never be poor again. Glory to God.

In the beginning of this book, we established the truth that we work to give. The reason being that our financial prosperity is more in our giving than our work. Work is important, it is the foundation of our prosperity but giving multiplies our finances.

The Bible says:

Eph 4:28 Let him that stole steal no more: but rather let him labour, working with his hands the thing which is good, that he may have to give to him that needeth.

Ephesians 4:28

This verse of scripture clearly tells us that the reason why we work is to give those in need. It is the primary reason why we work. So that we can be a blessing to others.

A worker that is not blessing others has missed the primary reason for working. If you are in such a place, you must align yourself quickly and become a giver.

I keep telling people that if you must fast so that you can give, then at all costs, do it.

That is where your next level of financial blessing is. Be a giver, it is why you work.

Financial seeds bring financial harvests

When you give, you have planted a financial seed and it will surely bring about a harvest far greater than the seed.

No one plants a grain of corn and expects a grain as harvest. The least you will get is about 100 grains of corn from that single grain of corn planted.

Your financial seeds also work that way. They come back to you multiplied. If you violate the law, you will grow poor. If you align yourself to the law, you will grow financially prosperous.

The Bible says that seedtime and harvest will never cease as long as the earth remains. You have a guaranteed law that will make sure your financial seeds are multiplied.

Gen 8:22 While the earth remaineth, seedtime and harvest, and cold and heat, and summer and winter, and day and night shall not cease.

Genesis 8:22

What are you waiting for beloved? Have a plan to start giving on a regular basis. There is multiplication of finances in your giving. Do not let such a great opportunity pass you by.

Many have thought themselves wise and missed this opportunity.

That shouldn't be your testimony. You are called out to prosper financially. Fulfil all righteousness as regards financial prosperity.

Types of giving

There are certain types of giving that must feature regularly in the life of everyone that wants to be financially prosperous. I will try to explain them as briefly as possible to help all those who need to know what they are.

No room enough to contain

The Bible tells us that there will not be room enough to contain the blessings those who tithe will receive.

This is huge. Yet regardless of this truth, some people are cheated out of tithing.

My dear, all you have was given to you by God. Giving Him a tenth of it must not be difficult. If you lose the life he gave you, you cannot make the money you think belongs to you.

Should you lose the eyes, legs and hands he gave you, you cannot earn what you are earning.

Every believer must understand that God is the one that made it possible to earn whatever you earn and so His honour must be given to Him.

Many people cannot be trusted by God. If He brings you $5000, he expects $500 to be given to your church or where you are fed the word of God as tithe.

If you cannot give a tithe of $500, do you expect more to be sent your way?

Look at the blessing of the principle of tithing and make a decision to be part of this blessing no matter what:

Mal 3:10 Bring ye all the tithes into the storehouse, that there may be meat in mine house, and prove me now herewith, saith the LORD of hosts, if I will not open you the windows

of heaven, and pour you out a blessing, that there shall not be room enough to receive it.

Mal 3:11 And I will rebuke the devourer for your sakes, and he shall not destroy the fruits of your ground; neither shall your vine cast her fruit before the time in the field, saith the LORD of hosts.

Malachi 3:10-11

Read this scripture carefully. Read it at least two times and tell me you do not want the blessing associated with tithing.

Do not be deceived.

Your faithfulness as a tither will open mighty doors for you and bring you many opportunities and ideas for multiplication and growth.

I have faithfully tithed and seen my finances grow over the years. Tithing doesn't make you poorer.

This you can attest yourself, as without tithing, you still have not prospered.

Offerings

Offerings are amounts you freely give to God. They are like financial seeds you sow. You give offerings to show how much you honour and appreciate God.

There is a promise of plenty as you give your offerings willingly.

Pro 3:9 Honour the LORD with thy substance, and with the firstfruits of all thine increase:

Pro 3:10 So shall thy barns be filled with plenty, and thy presses shall burst out with new wine.

Proverbs 3:9

Many people give their offerings anytime they are in church. It is a good avenue to be blessed financially.

Seeds

Seeds are given to meet special needs in your life.

There are many people who have needs that they do not have a harvest for.

Sowing seeds towards your marriage, your house, your children's education and so forth have proven to be powerful in the lives of many believers.

Do not relent in sowing towards these special seeds. The harvest come to meet such needs supernaturally.

2Co 9:10 Now he that ministereth seed to the sower both minister bread for your food, and multiply your seed sown, and increase the fruits of your righteousness;)

2 Corinthians 9:10

God will always give you seeds, be sure to sow them and not spend them.

Kingdom investments

One of the best places to sow is to sow in the kingdom of God.

Sponsoring crusades, outreaches, buildings and projects is a great way to multiply your finances as well as receive rewards in heaven.

Whatever you give for the kingdom, you are sure to have a hundred fold return here on earth, although **with persecution.**

Mar 10:29 And Jesus answered and said, Verily I say unto you, There is no man that hath left house, or brethren, or sisters, or father, or mother, or wife, or children, or lands, for my sake, and the gospel's,

Mar 10:30 But he shall receive an hundredfold now in this time, houses, and brethren, and sisters, and mothers, and children, and lands, with persecutions; and in the world to come eternal life.

Mark 10:30

Kingdom investment is never a waste but a great source of blessing both on earth and in heaven. It produces results in both places.

Men of God

When you give to men of God, you receive a special kind of blessing.

They can pronounce special blessings on you and they will be established. Many people have not tapped into this blessing, but it is scriptural.

The Bible says:

Mat 10:41 He that receiveth a prophet in the name of a prophet shall receive a prophet's reward; and he that receiveth a righteous man in the name of a righteous man shall receive a righteous man's reward.

Mat 10:42 And whosoever shall give to drink unto one of these little ones a cup of cold water only in the name of a disciple, verily I say unto you, he shall in no wise lose his reward.

Matthew 10:41-41

When Jacob brought Isaac the food to eat, Isaac blessed him after his soul was satisfied.

Giving to a man of God causes them to speak special blessings over your life. Let us do well to tap into this dimension of giving too.

Gen 27:4 And make me savoury meat, such as I love, and bring it to me, that I may eat; that my soul may bless thee before I die.

Genesis 27:4

Isaac took a meat offering and blessed Jacob before he died. The blessing of your man of God after giving to him works powerfully.

Giving to the poor

When we give to the poor, we lend to the Lord. As a believer, the Bible encourages you to give more to those in the kingdom who are in need.

Pro 19:17 He that hath pity upon the poor lendeth unto the LORD; and that which he hath given will he pay him again.

Proverbs 19:17

God says he will repay you when you give to the poor, hence giving to the poor is also good.

Giving to those in the household of faith is very important when prioritising your giving to those in need.

Gal 6:10 As we have therefore opportunity, let us do good unto all men, especially unto them who are of the household of faith.

Galatians 6:10

How to give

Many people have wondered how they should give.

The Bible is quite clear on how to go about this subject.

It says:

2Co 9:6 But this I say, He which soweth sparingly shall reap also sparingly; and he which soweth bountifully shall reap also bountifully.

2Co 9:7 Every man according as he purposeth in his heart, so let him give; not grudgingly, or of necessity: for God loveth a cheerful giver.

God expects us to give bountifully. Too many people are caught in the trap of giving the least amount they can give.

Such a manner of giving will affect what you reap. If you give sparingly, you will also reap sparingly. Thus if you want to prosper financially, learn to give bountifully so you can reap bountifully. It is a law and it has been working for you all along.

If you were giving sparingly, learn to start giving bountifully.

A word of advice to you is to ensure that you increase your giving periodically. Most people still give the same amount they gave 5 years ago. It will certainly affect what you receive as what you receive will also remain stagnant.

You must also give cheerfully. You must be happy that you are giving to no ordinary person but God almighty Himself.

You must thus have an attitude of cheerfulness when you give. After all you are going to receive far more than you give.

Let us move to the next chapter, where I will teach you how to increase your current financial level.

This same way is how you can decide to increase your future financial levels.

My desire is to see your progress and prosperity and freedom from negative people and circumstances. Because of that, please permit me to introduce two courses that I believe passionately will help you.

1. To cure prayerlessness, an inconsistent prayer life and the pain of not enjoying all that God has made available to you,, click here to learn more about my 3 Day Course on "How to Overcome prayerlessness" that will solve the problem of prayerlessness in your life.

2. To overcome the pain of not having enough money to live where you want, eat what you want to eat and be a blessing to the multitudes around you, I have created a 7 Day Financial Abundance

[Course](#) that will deliver financial abundance to you quickly.

Click [here](#) to learn more about that course.

You will see increase and enlargement as you step out in faith.

CHAPTER FIVE

CONCLUSION

In order to increase your current financial level, you must increase your input into any of the three parameters.

That is:

Increase your work or increase your knowledge or increase your giving.

Ideally, you can increase one or two or all three and the results will follow as you increase the parameters.

If you have made it this far, it means you are ready to receive massive financial increase. You are blessed.

My desire is to see your progress and prosperity and freedom from negative people and circumstances. Because of that, please permit me to introduce two courses that I believe passionately will help you.

1. To cure prayerlessness, an inconsistent prayer life and the pain of not enjoying all that God has made available to you,, click here to learn more about my 3 Day Course on "How to Overcome prayerlessness" that will solve the problem of prayerlessness in your life.

2. To overcome the pain of not having enough money to live where you want, eat what you want to eat and be a blessing to the multitudes around you, I have created a 7 Day Financial Abundance Course that will deliver financial abundance to you quickly.

Click here to learn more about that course.

You will see increase and enlargement as you step out in faith.

REVIEW

Because your review is important to help others benefit from these books, please leave a good review here

Please check out my other books on the next page

Other books by Francis Jonah

Other books by Francis Jonah

1. 3 Day Fasting Challenge: How to receive manifestation of answers

2. How to Have Outrageous Financial Abundance In No Time:Biblical Principles For Immediate And Overwhelming Financial Success

3. 5 Bible Promises, Prayers and Decrees That Will Give You The Best Year Ever: A book for Shaping Every Year Successfully plus devotional (Book Of Promises 1)

4. Influencing The Unseen Realm: How to Influence The Spirit Realm for Victory in The Physical Realm(Spiritual Success Books)

5. Prayer That Works: Taking Responsibility For Answered Prayer

6. Healing The Sick In Five Minutes: How Anyone Can Heal Any Sickness

7. The Financial Miracle Prayer

8. The Best Secret To Answered Prayer

9. [The Believer's Authority(Authority Of The Believer,Power And Authority Of The Believer)](#)

10. [The Healing Miracle Prayer](#)

11. [I Shall Not Die: Secrets To Long Life And Overcoming The Fear of Death](#)

12. [Three Straightforward Steps To Outrageous Financial Abundance: Personal Finance (Finance Made Easy Book 1)](#)

13. [Prayers For Financial Miracles: And 3 Ways To Receive Answers Quickly](#)

14. [Book: 3 Point Blueprint For Building Strong Faith: Spiritual:Religious:Christian:Motivational](#)

15. [How To Stop Sinning Effortlessly](#)

16. [The Power Of Faith-Filled Words](#)

17. [All Sin Is Paid For: An Eye Opening Book](#)

18. [Be Happy Now:No More Depression](#)

19. The Ultimate Christian: How To Win In Every Life Situation: A book full of Revelations

20. Books:How To Be Free From Sicknesses And Diseases(Divine Health): Divine Health Scriptures

21. Multiply Your Personal Income In Less Than 30 Days

22. Ultimate Method To Memorize The Bible Quickly: (How To Learn Scripture Memorization)

23. Overcoming Emotional Abuse

24. Passing Exams The Easy Way: 90% and above in exams (Learning Simplified)

25. Books:Goal Setting For Those In A Hurry To Achieve Fast

26. Do Something Lest You Do Nothing

27. Financial Freedom:My Personal Blue-Print Made Easy For Men And Women

28. Why Men Go To Hell

29. Budgeting Tools And How My Budget Makes Me More Money

30. How To Raise Capital In 72 Hours: Quickly and Effectively Raise Capital Easily in Unconventional Ways (Finance Made Easy)

31. How To Love Unconditionally

32. Financial Independence: The Simple Path I Used To Wealth

33. Finding Happiness: The Story Of John Miller: A Christian Fiction

34. Finance Made Easy (2 Book Series)

FREE GIFTS

Just to say Thank You for downloading my book, I'd like to give you these books for free.

Download these 4 powerful books today for free and give yourself a great future

Click Here Download

Your testimonies will abound. Click Here to see my other books. They have produced many testimonies and I want your testimony to be one too.

Printed in Great Britain
by Amazon